PROBLEM SOLVED!

YOUR TURN TO THINK BIG

Innovations in Communication

Cynthia O'Brien

Crabtree Publishing Company
www.crabtreebooks.com

![Crabtree logo]

Crabtree Publishing Company
www.crabtreebooks.com

Author: Cynthia O'Brien

Series research and development: Reagan Miller

Editorial director: Kathy Middleton

Editors: Crystal Sikkens, Janine Deschenes

Proofreader: Petrice Custance

Designer: Ken Wright

Cover design: Ken Wright

Photo researchers: Ken Wright, Crystal Sikkens

**Production coordinator
and prepress technician:** Ken Wright

Print coordinator: Katherine Berti

Cover: (top left) Guglielmo Marconi, inventor of the wireless telegraph; (top right) A space satellite in orbit; (bottom left) A laptop computer accessing the Internet; (bottom right) Teenagers texting each other

Title page: Illustration of Bell's photophone receiver

Photographs

Bridgeman Images: Beuzon, J. L. (fl.1933), p 4–5

Getty Images: Stefano Bianchetti, p 12–13 (bottom center); Michael Desmond/©ABC, p23

Library of Congress: p 24 (top right)

NASA: p 18 (top right)

Shutterstock: catwalker/ p14 (middle), p 27 (bkgd); Bloomicon, p 27 (forground)

Superstock: Science and Society, p 24 (bottom)

Wikimedia: cover (bkgd, bottom left and right inset), title page; p 7 (right); p 9; p 10 (bkgd); p 11; United States public domain, p 12 (left); Conklin, p 15; p 18 (bottom); p 20 (top right); p 22 (left middle); p 26 (top right)

All other images by Shutterstock

Library and Archives Canada Cataloguing in Publication

O'Brien, Cynthia (Cynthia J.), author
        Innovations in communication / Cynthia O'Brien.

(Problem solved! your turn to think big)
Includes index.
Issued in print and electronic formats.
ISBN 978-0-7787-2672-2 (hardback).--
ISBN 978-0-7787-2683-8 (paperback).--ISBN 978-1-4271-1804-2 (html)

        1. Communication--Technological innovations--Juvenile literature. 2. Telecommunication--Technological innovations--Juvenile literature. 3. Communication--Juvenile literature. 4. Telecommunication--Juvenile literature. 5. Inventions--Juvenile literature. I. Title.

P96.T42O27 2016   j384   C2016-904153-0
                                                         C2016-904154-9

Library of Congress Cataloging-in-Publication Data

Names: O'Brien, Cynthia (Cynthia J.), author.
Title: Innovations in communication / Cynthia O'Brien.
Description: New York, New York : Crabtree Publishing Company, [2016] | Series: Problem solved! Your turn to think big | Audience: Age 8-11. | Audience: Grades 4-6. | Includes index.
Identifiers: LCCN 2016026660 (print) | LCCN 2016029939 (ebook) | ISBN 9780778726722 (reinforced library binding) | ISBN 9780778726838 (pbk.) | ISBN 9781427118042 (Electronic HTML)
Subjects: LCSH: Telecommunication--Juvenile literature.
Classification: LCC TK5102.4 .O27 2016 (print) | LCC TK5102.4 (ebook) | DDC 384--dc23
LC record available at https://lccn.loc.gov/2016026660

Crabtree Publishing Company
www.crabtreebooks.com   1-800-387-7650

Printed in Canada/102016/IH20160811

**Published in Canada
Crabtree Publishing**
616 Welland Ave.
St. Catharines, Ontario
L2M 5V6

**Published in the United States
Crabtree Publishing**
PMB 59051
350 Fifth Avenue, 59th Floor
New York, New York 10118

**Published in the United Kingdom
Crabtree Publishing**
Maritime House
Basin Road North, Hove
BN41 1WR

**Published in Australia
Crabtree Publishing**
3 Charles Street
Coburg North
VIC, 3058

CONTENTS

Communication Changes

Imagine you want to say "Happy Birthday" to a friend who lives far away. You might call them on your phone, send a text message, or Skype. Now, imagine that phones and computers do not exist. Suddenly, saying "Happy Birthday" becomes a big problem! Luckily, people throughout history have solved these and other **communication** challenges.

Inventors and **innovators** solve a problem or meet a need. They have made our lives easier by finding different ways to help us communicate with each other. Today, we can send instant messages all over the world. In the future, even more ideas will change the way we communicate. Just think! It could be your chance to invent the next BIG thing!

Before phones and computers, sending a message to a friend could take days, weeks, or even longer. Today, messages can be sent instantly!

Inventions and Innovations

Inventors create products or processes no one has ever thought of before, such as the first computer. An innovation is an improvement or change to an invention that already exists. When computers were first invented, they were large and had to be used by many people at the same time. Through innovation, the company IBM created personal computers that could be used by one person at a time.

Engineers can also be inventors and innovators when they make new solutions or improve on existing ones. An engineer's job is to use science and math to solve problems or meet needs. Inventors, innovators, and engineers all share the same **traits**, such as curiosity and creativity.

The first personal computers were similar to the ones you use today!

Read All About It!

You've seen shelves of books in your local library, school, and for sale in stores. But, it wasn't always this easy for people to get a book to read. There was a time when books were very rare. People called **scribes** had to write and copy books by hand! This took a long time and made books very expensive.

Gutenberg's wooden printing press used ink and raised letters, called type, to print its pages.

The Printing Press

In about 1450 A.D., Johannes Gutenberg invented the printing press—a machine that printed one page every three minutes. That's a lot faster than writing by hand! Imagine what Gutenberg would think of the speedy printing presses we have now. Today's printers can make thousands of books, newspapers, magazines, and more in no time at all.

In 1971, Martin Hart came up with the idea of e-books. Inspired by Gutenberg, he named his digital library of e-books Project Gutenberg. Today, people read e-books on computers, tablets, or other devices.

Communicating without Sight

Imagine if there were no books for you to read! Louis Braille was blind from the age of three. When he was growing up, there were no books for people who were blind. Braille wanted to change this. When he was 11 years old, Braille met Charles Barbier de la Serre, who had invented a code of raised dots for soldiers to communicate in the dark. Over the next three years, Braille improved upon Barbier de la Serre's invention and created his own system of raised dots that allowed blind people to read. He published the first Braille book in 1829. Since then, Braille's innovation has spread around the world.

BRAILLE Alphabet

A B C D E F G H I
J K L M N O P Q R
S T U V W X Y Z

? ! ' - CAPITAL # 0

1 2 3 4 5 6 7 8 9

Braille's system uses combinations of six raised dots. Each combination is assigned to a different letter or punctuation mark. There is now Braille code for most languages, as well as music and math.

Young Inventor Spotlight

Shubham Banerjee

You can now buy keyboards for computers with the Braille code on them. However, buying printers that print in braille can be expensive. Shubham Banerjee, an eighth grade student in California, used LEGO® to make a low-cost Braille printer to make Braille printing more affordable. Shubham's printer is **portable**, and easily connects to a computer.

Going the Distance

How do you get in touch with people? Do you use a phone, or a computer? If you lived 200 years ago, you would have sent a letter. It could take weeks or even months for your message to arrive! A few people started thinking about ways to send messages quicker. Samuel Morse and his partners, Leonard Gale and Alfred Vail, came up with a machine that used electricity to send signals along a wire. They called it the electric telegraph. Morse and Vail then developed the **Morse code** so people could understand the signals. Soon, telegraph cables crisscrossed around the world. The telegraph connected people like never before.

Morse code is a system that matches long and short signals of light or sound with letters.

Young Inventor Spotlight

Arsh Shah Dilbagi

Teenager Arsh Shah Dilbagi wanted to find a way to connect people who cannot speak. People who cannot speak often use sign language. Dilbagi designed TALK to help them speak over long distances, when face-to-face sign language isn't possible. Using his invention, people breathe in long or short breaths according to the Morse code. TALK translates their breaths into words!

The telegraph was used around the world, but could only send signals. Inventors wanted to know if they could create a "talking telegraph" to **transmit** spoken messages, too. The first person to come up with an idea was Antonio Meucci. He showed his machine to friends and business people. However, Meucci was very poor and could not afford a **patent** to give him ownership of the idea.

In 2002, the United States Congress recognized Meucci's work on the telephone.

Sending Messages

About ten years later, Alexander Graham Bell and Elisha Gray started working on machines. Bell eventually received a patent and obtained all the rights to make and sell the telephone. Even though Elisha Gray did not win the patent for the telephone, he didn't stop inventing. He held over 70 patents for his many inventions. One of his later inventions was the telautograph. This machine could send handwritten notes and simple drawings across distances!

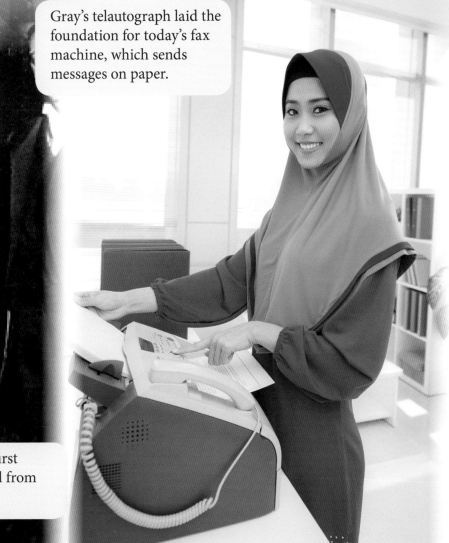

Gray's telautograph laid the foundation for today's fax machine, which sends messages on paper.

In 1892, Bell made the first long-distance phone call from New York to Chicago.

Look! No Wires!

Telegraphs and early telephones needed expensive cables to work. It was sometimes impossible to build cable systems in certain places. Inventor Guglielmo Marconi changed all that. He designed the "wireless," or the radio. This new invention allowed people to send messages without wires. Before long, radio stations were **broadcasting** news, plays, and music.

The next time you listen to a radio, remember to thank Guglielmo Marconi.

Life saver

Marconi's invention of the radio also helped save lives! In 1909, two ships collided. The RMS *Republic* began to sink and sent out a radio message. Other ships heard the message and rushed to help. The ships rescued over 1,500 people. Without the radio, the ships would not have been able to communicate with each other.

The RMS *Republic* collided with the SS *Florida* (right). Fortunately, the damage to the SS *Florida* wasn't enough to cause it to leak. It returned to help rescue survivors from the crash.

Young Inventor Spotlight — Sophie Swingle

In 2010, teenager Sophie Swingle used similar radio technology to design a life-saving device. Sophie saw a news report about miners trapped underground in Utah. The miners did not have a way to communicate with the rescue workers above ground. To solve this problem, Sophie designed a handheld device that can transmit a **distress** signal 500 feet (152 meters) through the earth.

Type it Up

You probably write some of your homework with a pencil or pen. Imagine writing a whole book that way! People used to do that all the time. Christopher Latham Sholes was a printer and newspaper editor who wanted to make his job easier. With the help of two other inventors, he created the first typewriter. Sholes's invention changed the way that everyone wrote—even today.

Instead of arranging the letters on the typewriter by the alphabet, Sholes decided to place them in a way so the keys wouldn't jam. Our computer keyboards are set up this same way.

Talking Type

Some people who have physical disabilities are unable to type on a computer. Luckily, Lenny Baum and other scientists developed a voice **recognition** system. Now, people can talk into the computer system and their voices are turned into words on the screen! This makes it much easier for people of all abilities to use a computer to communicate.

Voice recognition systems are useful for people who have physical disabilities, as well as people who are blind, who are learning a new language, and who have learning disabilities such as **dyslexia**.

Working Together

What do you do if you can't think of a way to solve a problem? You ask someone for help! Some of the best ideas come when we work as a team. This happened at Bell Laboratories. For almost 100 years, the company has brought together many scientists and engineers that have come up with amazing inventions and innovations. One of these was the communications **satellite**.

The first communication satellite was called Telstar 1. It was launched into space in 1962.

How does it work?

Do you talk or text on a cell phone, watch television, or use the Internet? If you do, you're probably using a satellite. Bell Labs created the world's first two-way communications satellite. Pictures, sound, and information from Earth are sent to satellites in space. Then, the satellite sends these signals to other places around the world.

Today, over 1,000 two-way communications satellites orbit, or circle, Earth.

Young Inventor Spotlight

Josua Nghaamwa

Josua Nghaamwa lives in Africa. Many African people live in small villages. It can be difficult for them to connect to the Internet. To help this problem, Josua made a satellite booster. The booster helps to make the satellite signal stronger outside of cities, so that Internet access can be made available to a larger number of people.

Cell Phones

You may not have a cell phone, but you probably know someone who does. The first call on a cell phone was made by engineer Martin Cooper in April 1973. He called Bell Labs! The first cell phones were very expensive, and about the size of a brick! Luckily, innovators found ways to make phones smaller and cheaper. Some cell phones, known as smartphones, are like small computers.

Most cell phones today are built with cameras, games, and a lot more. With your help, the next new thing could be just around the corner.

MERRY CHRISTMAS!

A text is a short, written message. Matti Makkonen, an engineer from Finland, helped to invent this quick way of communicating. In 1992, Neil Papworth figured out how to send the first text. He sent the message "Merry Christmas" to his boss.

MERRY CHRISTMAS!
NEIL

Today, people send and receive millions of texts every day.

Polaroid camera

Pictures can share ideas and information as a form of visual communication. It's easy to take and share pictures with digital cameras and cell phones. Before they existed however, it took a long time for people to see the pictures they took. That changed in 1943 when Edwin Land took some pictures while on vacation with his family. His daughter asked why they couldn't see the pictures they took right away. This got Edwin thinking that there must be a way to see the pictures faster. Before long, he had invented the first instant camera. He called it the Polaroid Land camera. This amazing new device could develop and print the film in just a minute!

Young Inventor Spotlight

Brooke Martin

Brooke Martin knew her dog missed her when she wasn't home. She decided to use the cameras on her family's devices to connect with him all day! When she was only 12 years old, Brooke invented the iCPooch to make sure her dog felt loved. Using Brooke's device, dogs can see and hear their owners through the screen of the device!

Using Brooke's invention, owners can talk to their dogs from anywhere. They can even press a button to give their dog a treat!

Video chat with your dog and deliver a treat from anywhere!
iCPooch

Information at Your Fingertips

Imagine what your life would be like without computers! How would you complete a school project, or connect with friends? It was inventor Charles Babbage that came up with the first idea of an automatic digital computer in the 1800s. Babbage's computer didn't look anything like computers today, however. The plans for his programmable mechanical computer showed it would be able to perform, store, and print mathematical calculations and tables, as well as follow instructions. Unfortunately, Babbage was never able to finish building his machine.

In 1991, British scientists used Babbage's plans to complete his computer, called the Analytical Engine. A model of the machine is shown at left.

Powerful Chip

Many years later, the first useable computers were built. However, these computers were so big, that they took up entire rooms! People needed special training to use them. Life became much easier when personal computers, or PCs, were invented. PCs were developed after Ted Hoff designed the **microprocessor**, a tiny chip that contains all the functions of a huge computer. It didn't take long for PCs to become very popular. Ted Hoff's invention paved the way for many other ideas, including the computers you use today. What do you think the PC of the future will look like?

Microprocessors are everywhere, from laptops and smartphones to washing machines and DVD players.

Connecting the World

If you had one of the first computers, you wouldn't be able to use it to communicate with your friends and family. Computers could hold information, but there was no way to share it with others! This changed when computer scientists developed the Internet. The Internet is a **network** that connects one computer or device to another. When you connect to the Internet, you can find millions of websites. Websites start with the letters "www." This stands for the World Wide Web, an information space that holds all of the websites.

The World Wide Web is the invention of a computer scientist named Tim Berners-Lee.

Facebook

Today, the World Wide Web allows you to use social media websites, such as Facebook, to connect with friends and family all over the world! Mark Zuckerberg founded Facebook in 2004. It is a site where you can send and share news and pictures with friends and family.

Zuckerberg's Facebook website is one of the most popular social media sites in the world. More than one billion people use it!

Now it's Your Turn!

Inventors, innovators, and engineers follow a set of steps to solve problems and meet needs. These steps are called the Engineering Design Process. The steps in the process can be repeated as many times as needed.

Ask
What is a problem I want to solve or a need I want to meet?

Brainstorm
Write down all possible solutions.

Plan
Choose the best solution. Write a list of the steps you will follow and materials you will need. Sketch your design.

Create
Build a solution using your plan. Test to see how well it works.

Improve and Communicate
Review your results. Keep improving and testing your solution. Share your results with others.

28

Think Big!

Communication can be done through speech, written words, or pictures. The ways that we communicate and connect with each other haven't stopped changing. Over time, inventors, innovators, and engineers have given us incredible new ways to communicate.

How do you communicate with people around you? Could there be a faster, safer, or more interesting way to connect? Maybe there is a way to improve an invention that already exists—or you might think of something totally new! Get your inventor's mind going. What could be the next big communications idea?

Think about a problem you would like to solve or a need you would like to meet. Or choose one of these communication challenges:

- Helping people with disabilities communicate more easily, such as people who are blind or deaf
- Sending a message in a new or different way
- Is there a safer or more secure way to connect with people online?
- Is there a faster way to communicate with others?

Follow the steps in the Engineering Design Process to think big and solve your problem!

Learning More

Books:

Bozzo, Linda. *Staying in Touch in the Past, Present, and Future.* Bailey Books, 2010

Casey, Susan. *Kids Inventing! A Handbook for Young Inventors.* Jossey-Bass, 2005

Graham, Ian. *Communication.* QEB, 2008

Hegedus, Alannah and Kaitlin Rainey. *Bleeps and Blips to Rocket Ships: Great Inventions in Communications.* Tundra, 2001

Websites:

This site has biographies, stories, and information about the history of the telecommunications industry:
www.telcomhistory.org/vm/scienceBeforePhones.shtml

Visit this site for biographies of award-winning young inventors. It includes games, resources, and information to encourage aspiring young inventors:
http://lemelson.mit.edu/

Find out more about communications-related inventions and their inventors here:
www.enchantedlearning.com/inventors/communication.shtml

Glossary

broadcast To make something available to the public through radio, television, or online

communication The use of words, sounds, signs, or actions to share infomation

distress To be in danger

dyslexia A condition that makes it difficult for someone to read, write, or spell

engineer A person with scientific training who designs and builds complicated products, machines, systems, or structures

innovator A person who improves, adapts, or enhances an existing invention

inventor A person who first comes up with a brand new idea, product, process, or device

microprocessor A device in a computer that manages information and controls what the computer does

Morse code A system of sending messages using long and short sounds, flashes of light, or marks to represent letters and numbers

network A system of computers and other devices that are connected to each other

patent An official document that gives a person or company the right to be the only one that makes or sells a product

portable Something that is easily carried or moved around

recognition To know who someone is, or what something is, because you have seen them before

satellite A machine that is sent into space

scribe A person who writes or copies documents by hand

traits Qualities or characteristics that belong to a person

transmit To send information through electronic signals

INDEX

About the Author

Cynthia O'Brien writes non-fiction for children and adults. After working in children's publishing in London, England, for several years, she decided to return to Canada and turn her attention to writing. Cynthia lives in Guelph.